CELEBRATING ADVENT
with the Jesse Tree

REV. JUDE WINKLER, OFM Conv.

Imprimi Potest: Daniel Pietrzak, OFM Conv., Minister Provincial of St. Anthony of Padua Province (USA)
Nihil Obstat: James T. O'Connor, S.T.D., Censor Librorum
Imprimatur: ✠ **Patrick J. Sheridan, D.D.**, Vicar General, Archdiocese of New York

PREPARING FOR CHRISTMAS

CHRISTMAS is one of the happiest days of the year. It is the day when we celebrate how much God loves us. We rejoice because God sent His only Son into our world to be born as a baby in Bethlehem.

Because it is such an important day, there are many things we have to do to prepare for it. Months before it arrives we begin to think about the presents that we will receive from our parents. We must ask to go to the toy store or talk to our friends to decide what we should ask them to buy for us.

As the day approaches, there are all kinds of preparations to do at home. We help Dad and Mom get ready for our celebration. We help them clean the house, bake cookies, decorate the Christmas tree, and all the other things that have to be done. There is really a lot to do to get ready for Christmas.

Yet, we have to be careful that we do not spend all our time preparing our homes and then forget to prepare our hearts. That is why we have a special time of the year called Advent. It is when we look at our hearts to make sure that we are ready to welcome the baby Jesus into our lives and our love.

THE JESSE TREE

ADVENT is a good time to think back on how God prepared the hearts of His people for the birth of His only Son. That way, when we have heard how they grew closer to God all throughout their history, we might be encouraged to draw close to God ourselves.

It would be impossible to look at every single thing that God did for His people before Jesus was born, but maybe we can look at a few of those things. We will be looking at the Jesse tree. This is the name given to the promises that God made throughout the Old Testament concerning the birth of His only Son.

Just like our Christmas tree, the Jesse tree has beautiful decorations. But instead of having stars and lights on it, it has the promises that God made to us and to His people, promises made out of love.

The tree is named after Jesse, the father of David, the great king of Israel. The reason for this is that some of the most important promises of all were made to Jesse and to his son David. They were promised that God's only Son would be born in their family.

GOD CREATES ADAM AND EVE

THE first branch of this tree is very old, for it dates back all the way to the first days of the world.

In the beginning God created the heavens and the earth and all the things that are in them. The greatest of all the things that He created were the first man and woman. God loved Adam and Eve and He put them in charge of all His creation.

God placed Adam and Eve in the Garden of Eden. He told them that they could eat the fruit of any tree in the garden except the tree of the knowledge of good and evil. They were not to eat the fruit of that tree.

One day, while Eve was walking in the garden, a serpent spoke to her and convinced her to eat some of the fruit that she was not supposed to eat. When she had tasted the fruit, she gave some to Adam, her husband. As soon as they finished, they realized that they had sinned against God.

When God came to walk in the garden that evening, they hid from Him, for they knew that they had done something very bad. He called them out from hiding and spoke to them.

THE PROMISE OF A SAVIOR

WHEN they finally came out, God told the man, the woman, and the serpent that they would be punished for the bad thing they had done. He told the man that from then on he would have to work very hard to earn a living for his family. He told the woman that she would be punished by having much pain when she was giving birth to her children.

God gave the most serious punishment to the serpent for it had tempted the woman to turn against the Lord. He told it that it would no longer have any legs but would have to crawl on its belly for the rest of its life.

One part of the punishment is actually a promise to us. God told the serpent that the child of the woman would step on the head of the serpent. This was a promise that the devil would not be powerful forever. God was promising to send a Holy One who would crush the power of the evil one and free us from sin.

Then, to show us that He still loved Adam and Eve and all of us in spite of our sins, He made some clothes for Adam and Eve to protect them from the cold. This is the story of God's first promise to send Jesus into the world.

NOAH AND THE FLOOD

I N spite of the love that God had shown Adam and Eve, men and women continued to turn against the Lord. They sinned more and more until God finally decided that He would have to punish the whole world.

God decided that He would send a great flood to destroy all life upon the earth. He would only save one very good family from the flood, Noah and his family.

One day God called to Noah and told him to build a large boat, an ark. When he was finished, he was to collect all kinds of animals and to put them on board the ark. Noah did just as the Lord commanded him.

When Noah was finished and had all the animals on board the ark, God sent a great flood that destroyed all people and animals upon the earth. The flood lasted a long time, but all throughout it God kept Noah and his family safe.

Then, when the flood was over, God promised Noah that He would never again flood the whole earth. He gave us the rainbow as a sign of His promise. Once again, in spite of the fact that we had sinned, God gave us a sign of His mercy and His love.

ABRAHAM AND SARAH

THE next branch on our Jesse tree is the promise that God made to Abraham and Sarah. God promised that, even though they were very old, they would still have a son. Their children and grandchildren and other descendants would be as many as the stars in the sky. He also promised them a fertile land in which they could dwell.

Abraham and Sarah waited for a long time, but still they had no children. Then, one day, God visited them along with two angels in the form of three desert travelers. Abraham and Sarah were so kind and generous to them that God repeated His promise and then added that He would fulfill it within one year. Sarah soon became pregnant and gave birth to a son, Isaac.

Some time later, God asked Abraham to give Isaac back to Him in sacrifice. Although Abraham could have wondered whether God was taking back His promise, he trusted God. When God saw Abraham's great faith, He stopped him from sacrificing his son and greatly rewarded Abraham and Sarah. They were to become the father and the mother of God's holy people, Israel. It would be to this people that God would send His only Son, Jesus.

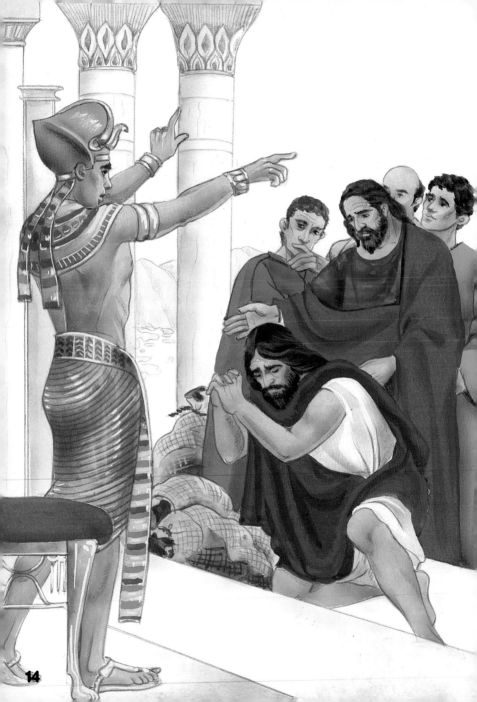

THE SONS OF JACOB

GOD continued to fulfill His promise to Abraham and Sarah. Isaac, their son, married Rebekah and they had two sons, Esau and Jacob. God chose Jacob as the son of His promise. Jacob and his wives, Leah and Rachel, had twelve sons and one daughter.

These twelve sons were to become the founders of the twelve tribes of Israel. Two of the most famous sons were Joseph and Judah.

Joseph was one of the youngest sons and he was a favorite of his father. His brothers hated him for that and sold him into slavery in Egypt. God cared for him there and made him an important official in the court of Pharaoh, the king of Egypt. When a great famine broke out over all the earth, Joseph was able to give grain to his family and to save them from death. He forgave his brothers and brought them and their father Jacob to Egypt where they could live in safety.

Judah, the second oldest son, was to become famous because of a promise that Jacob made to his son before he died. He told Judah that he would be as strong as a lion and would be the father of great kings. One day, the King of kings, Jesus, would be born from his tribe.

MOSES THE LIBERATOR

THE people of Israel grew very strong in Egypt, so strong that the Egyptians became frightened of them. They made them into slaves and treated them very badly.

God heard the cries of His people and He sent them a prophet, Moses, to lead them to freedom. Moses told Pharaoh to let his people go, and when Pharaoh refused, God sent a series of plagues against Egypt. Finally, God sent a terrible plague in which all the first sons of Egypt died, and Pharaoh let the people of Israel go.

When the army of Pharaoh chased after the people of Israel, God had Moses part the Red Sea and lead the people across. He drowned Pharaoh and his army in the Red Sea.

Israel dwelt in the desert for forty years. God cared for them there, giving them bread from heaven, which is called manna, and water from a rock. He also gave them a gift through Moses, the Ten Commandments, so that they would know how to serve God and to love each other. Before he died, Moses promised that God would send another prophet greater than he ever was. That prophet was Jesus, God's only Son.

YOUR GOD WILL BE MY GOD

ONE of those who was part of God's promise was Ruth, a woman from a foreign land.

There was a good woman from Israel named Naomi who moved from her home in Bethlehem to Moab, a pagan land, with all of her family. While she was there, her two sons married women from Moab. Eventually her husband died as well as her two sons. She told her two daughters-in-law that they should return to their families and she would return to Jerusalem.

One of the daughters-in-law returned to her family, but Ruth, the other one, refused to do this. She told Naomi that she would go with her wherever she went. Naomi's people would be her people and Naomi's God would be her God.

Naomi and Ruth traveled to Bethlehem. When they arrived there, Ruth cared for Naomi by picking up the loose grain in the fields that had been harvested. God rewarded Ruth for her goodness to Naomi. He sent a good man of Israel, Boaz, into her life. They married and had a son named Obed, who was to be the grandfather of David, the great king of Israel. Thus, Ruth was also one of the ancestors of Jesus, our Lord.

DAVID, THE SON OF JESSE

GOD does not always make the same choices that we would probably make, and this is seen most clearly in the story of David.

The people of Israel had asked God and the prophet Samuel for a king, and God had given them Saul. But Saul did things that were evil in the sight of God, so God told the prophet Samuel that he should go out and anoint a new king.

Samuel traveled to Bethlehem, to the house of Jesse, as God had ordered. He told Jesse to bring all his sons before him. But as each son passed in front of him, Samuel knew that the Lord was not choosing that man to be the future king of Israel.

When all Jesse's sons had passed in front of the prophet, Samuel asked Jesse if there were any others. Jesse said that the youngest son, David, was out tending sheep. Samuel had him called, and the minute he saw David he knew that God had chosen him.

God chose David not because he was the oldest or the tallest or the most handsome. He chose him because he was pure of heart, for God judges us according to our hearts. So Samuel took out his oil and anointed David the king of Israel.

A HOUSE FOR DAVID

DAVID became a great hero in Israel. He defeated the giant Goliath and many of the other enemies who were attacking his people. Then, when king Saul was killed in battle, David became the king of all of Israel.

One of the first things that David did as king was to capture the city of Jerusalem and to make it his capital. He built a great palace for himself. He also brought the Ark of the Covenant, the holiest of all the things that God had given to His people, into Jerusalem.

One day David called Nathan the prophet to his palace. David told Nathan that he felt guilty, for here he was living in a great palace while the Ark of the Covenant was still in a tent. He wanted to build a great temple to house the Ark.

God spoke to Nathan, sending him to speak to David. Nathan told David that God did not want him to build Him a house. Rather, God was going to give David a house that would never end.

This was a promise that David's descendants would rule over Israel for all time. It would be fulfilled when Jesus, the son of David, would become the King of Israel and the King of all kings.

EMMANUEL

THE descendants of David, however, did not follow the Lord with all their hearts. So God sent them prophets to call them back to His ways.

One of the prophets whom God sent was Isaiah. The people of Israel had sinned against the Lord and God had allowed their enemies to attack them. God then sent Isaiah to the king and told him to trust in the Lord, for God would defeat all of Israel's enemies.

Isaiah told the king to ask for a sign from the Lord as an assurance that they would be delivered, but the king refused to ask for a sign. The prophet told the king that God would give a sign anyway, for a maiden would bear a child who would be named Emmanuel, a name that means "God is with us."

The prophet also promised that when this child would reign, there would be a time a peace in Israel and over the whole world. The peace would be so great that even the wolf would lie down with the lamb and the lion with the calf. There would be a great peace on God's holy mountain. Jesus is the fulfillment of this promise, for He truly is "God with us"; He truly is the Prince of Peace.

LITTLE TOWN OF BETHLEHEM

S TILL the kings who lived in Jerusalem continued to sin against the Lord. And so God sent another prophet, Micah, who would make still another promise to the people of Israel.

Micah realized that the people of Jerusalem had forgotten the Lord. They were too rich and too important, so they did not have time to pray or to turn to the Lord. They were not humble enough to admit that they needed God's help.

But people of the small towns were always turning to God. Micah saw this and realized that the poor people and the unimportant are really the chosen ones of God. He remembered how God had chosen David, a small and unimportant child from Bethlehem, to be His great king.

So Micah spoke to Bethlehem and promised that another King would arise out of it. This King would reign over Israel just as David had done. He would be pleasing to God and turn all the people back to justice. He would rule forever.

When the Magi came to Herod to ask where the new King of Israel was born, the wise men of Israel turned to this promise to tell Herod that the Messiah was to be born in Bethlehem.

A NEW JERUSALEM

EVEN though God had sent many Prophets to Israel to turn His people away from their sins, they refused to listen to them. Finally, God sent a terrible punishment upon His people. He allowed the enemies of Israel to conquer the land and to take them off into exile.

The people of Israel were now living in a foreign land, and they began to wonder whether God had forgotten them or whether He was taking back His promises to them. God sent them a number of Prophets to reassure them that this was not the case.

These Prophets spoke of how God would restore His beloved land. He would build a new Jerusalem that would be much better than the one that had been destroyed. He would give His people a time of peace and prosperity.

God also promised that He would send one of His servants to His people. This Servant would preach the Word of God to all the nations and turn their hearts to the Lord. He would suffer for the sake of the people and take their sins upon Himself. He would die for His people, and then the Lord would raise Him from the dead. That Servant of the Lord was Jesus Himself.

JOHN THE BAPTIST

THE people of Israel tried to believe in the promises that God had made, but they waited for a long time and suffered a great deal.

Then, one day, a priest named Zechariah was in the temple burning incense before the altar of God. An angel appeared to him and told him that he and his wife, Elizabeth, would soon have a son. They were to name their son John and he would be a powerful messenger of the Lord. He would turn the people back to the Lord and prepare them for the coming of the Messiah.

Zechariah and Elizabeth were both very old, and Zechariah wondered how this could happen. The angel Gabriel replied that he had been sent from God Himself. Because Zechariah had doubted the promise of the Lord, he would be unable to speak until the child was born.

Zechariah returned to his home and soon afterward Elizabeth became pregnant. In her pregnancy she was helped by her cousin, the Virgin Mary, who was to be the Mother of God's Son, Jesus. The son whom Elizabeth bore was John the Baptist who would go out into the desert and baptize the people so that they might be ready to greet Jesus with their whole hearts.

THE JESSE TREE

DURING the Season of Advent we can think of the people and events of the Jesse Tree.

First Week — Numbers 1, 2, and 3
Second Week — Numbers 4, 5, and 6
Third Week — Numbers 7, 8, and 9
Fourth Week — Numbers 10 and 11

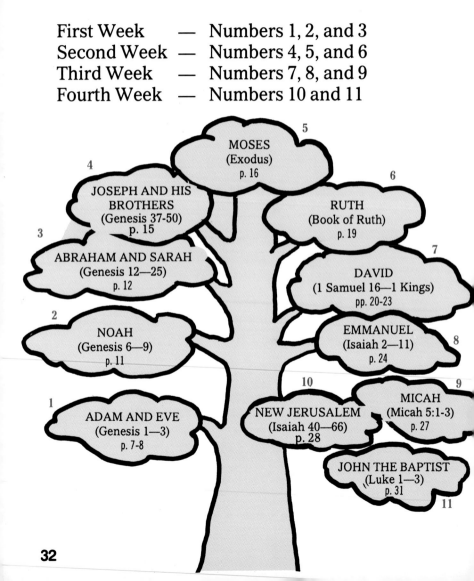

5 MOSES (Exodus) p. 16

4 JOSEPH AND HIS BROTHERS (Genesis 37-50) p. 15

6 RUTH (Book of Ruth) p. 19

3 ABRAHAM AND SARAH (Genesis 12—25) p. 12

7 DAVID (1 Samuel 16—1 Kings) pp. 20-23

2 NOAH (Genesis 6—9) p. 11

EMMANUEL (Isaiah 2—11) p. 24 8

10 NEW JERUSALEM (Isaiah 40—66) p. 28

9 MICAH (Micah 5:1-3) p. 27

1 ADAM AND EVE (Genesis 1—3) p. 7-8

JOHN THE BAPTIST (Luke 1—3) p. 31 11